DAY 1

Sometimes when you win, you really lose. And sometimes when you lose, you really win. And sometimes when you win or lose, you actually tie. And sometimes when you tie, you actually lose. Winning or losing is all one organic mechanism, from which one extracts what one needs.

| |
| |
| |
| |
| |
| |
| |
| |
| |

DON'T FORGET YOUR FATHER

A few years ago my children were both mid-teens. My Son was 15 years old and my Daughter was 16 years old. At the time, my Son was living with his biological Mother and his Stepfather seven states away and my Daughter was here with my Wife and I. It was a rough patch for me with communication for both kids. I called and text to talk with my Son daily; no interaction back. How? When our time together throughout his entire life was special and heart filled. My daughter and I spoke every day, pretty well and always had great communication filled with trust. However, she did not keep the lines of communication positive with her biological Father as she should have. How? She knows how much it hurts for me not to talk to her Brother every day. She knows how often I would ask her to reach out to her biological Father, just because.

What I realized is that I cannot be this great motivational speaker, mentor, life coach, workshop specialist, effective communicator guy and not do something to show them both how just an intentional 2minute thought could go a long way. I figured I'd just show them! With that, I decided that every day for one year, a whole 365 days, I would text them an inspirational thought or quote of some sort. No excuses! 365 days straight! I told them that I would send them the individual text without any expectation or requested response, simply to show a form of love through communication. The goal was to show them how to be intentional and live up to what you commit yourself to someone you love.

A lot of these quotes are quotes from other people – some famous, some not, some close to me and some just off various friends on social media post. Keep in mind, some are my original thoughts, straight from the heart.

I hope that you can enjoy this journey with me. I hope that something resonates with you. I hope that something grows you to the next level of your life. And I hope that you grow closer to your own children or loved ones through my downfalls.

Enjoy!

"Your network is your net'worth'"
-BJ Paige

A Poem from me to my children:

I know it's a lot going on in one way or another
I'll never try to bridge a wedge between you and your
Mother
It's just that I remember holding you in my arms when you
were small
Now as you grow tall it's hard to explain how I'm here if you
ever fall
And that I never had an instruction manual to show me any
other way
Or even a good male example for when I was your age to
help me day to day
What I do know is that I love you and will forever be in your
corner
When times are good or bad, to cheer you on or just to warn
ya
To hug you, to listen, never to judge you for what you want
to do
And be sure when you have children, I'm their PaPa to help
you through
Times like this, the feelings I have now, you won't ever have
to bother
Worrying if your children have to be told "Don't Forget Your
Father"

This group of inspirational quotes are meant for you to read one each day for 365 days straight. I welcome you to share this with your children and loved ones each day. Write down what you feel or what you're thinking of at the time each day. There will be days where these quotes will be right on time for what you are going through with you and your family. You never know how much it could change your life or your relationship with your family. What I realized is, as I began to offer these each day to my children, I was helping myself heal......I was growing a new me. Not saying that the old me was not good but hey, we all need that extra push every now and then, we all will forever continue to grow. My wish is that we all grow in a positive manner.

From my family to yours, be blessed and live life, leading with love!

DAY 2

Yesterday's score can't win today's game!!
Win today!!!

DAY 3

Luck Is What Happens When Preparation Meets Opportunity

DAY 4

You can repay people, including
yourself, with anything –
money, love, food, etc. You can't repay
people for their time.
You can't ever get that time back, use it
wisely

_____

DAY 5

There's a big difference between being tired,
being sleepy and being lazy

DAY 6

Sometimes things happen for a reason
or a season,
but sometimes things happen as a
lesson

DAY 7

Some people don't need costumes to
dress up for Halloween

DAY 8

STOP - Seek Time Or Pay - Seek the time today to make your tomorrow just that much better

-BJ Paige

DAY 9

A plan without action is a dream
without a thought

DAY 10

Sometimes we don't even see why
things happen,
but we always see the results

| |
| |
| |
| |
| |
| |
| |
| |

DAY 11

If you stay ready, you don't have to get ready

Day 12

It's easy to try hard every day when you understand why you're working hard every day....find your why!

DAY 13

There's only one thing that you're in
control of, that's you!
Stay in control!

DAY 14

Habits are formed, do something long enough and it's becomes a part of your habits...be careful what you do on a daily

DAY 15

Make sure you enjoy the smell of the cookies while they are baking in the oven, you will always remember that smell

DAY 16

Games are fun to play, and they all have rules...you can pause, quit and start over at any time; life is not a game, don't play with it

_____

_____
_____
_____
_____
_____
_____
_____

DAY 17

Remember, a safe plane can't land until
the coast is clear. Make sure you clean
up your landing strip on the ground
where you are

DAY 18

Time is so precious, if time were money
would you manage it better?

_____
_____
_____
_____
_____
_____
_____
_____

DAY 19

There's piece and then there's
peace....know the difference and focus
when you need them both!

DAY 20

Be careful what you watch on TV aka the television.....
it tells, u, a, vision....

DAY 21

Make sure you listen when people talk.
We always hear what people say but
listening is different,
you accept what you are listening to

DAY 22

Remember the importance of giving
back,
it's a way to help the sun shine on you

| |
| |
| |
| |
| |
| |
| |
| |

DAY 23

If you're absence doesn't affect them,
then their presence really didn't matter

DAY 24

Learn from the mistakes of others,
you can't live long enough to make
them all yourself

DAY 25

The distance between dreams and
reality is called action

DAY 26

Do better until you know better and when
you know better
make sure you do better

DAY 27

Today make sure to not just be thankful but be grateful for all that you have and not for what you don't have

DAY 28

Sometimes your best teacher is the last
mistake you made

DAY 29

Your mind is like your bed, you have to
make it up every day
and be careful who you let in it

DAY 30

Expect to be great because that's what
you are

DAY 32

Your competition isn't other people, it's your procrastination

DAY 33

The worst lie is the lie to yourself

DAY 34

Find what you're good at, make
yourself great at it and that's what you
need to do for the rest of your life

DAY 35

If you have no success you have no critics

DAY 36

Sometimes you have to put aside what
you feel for people and pay attention to
their actions, that's how they feel for
you

.

DAY 37

The best way to predict the future is to
create it

DAY 38

Change your thinking, or you'll recycle
the same experiences
over and over

DAY 39

Some people cross your path and change
your whole direction

DAY 40

Don't mistake silence for a weakness,
smart people don't plan big moves

DAY 41

The biggest battle in life is the now you
vs. the old you

DAY 42

Stop getting distracted by the things
that have
nothing to do with your goals

DAY 43

You don't have to learn how to control
your thoughts,
you have to learn how to not let them
control you

DAY 44

Most of the time we don't get what we
want
until we become the type of person
who should receive it

DAY 45

Never complain about what you lost,
be thankful for what you already have

DAY 46

Don't let a bad day make you feel like
you have a bad life

DAY 47

Never be too proud to ask a winner
how to win

DAY 48

Don't ever dim your light to make
others feel comfortable

DAY 49

If you woke up today without at least
one goal to do,
go back to sleep

DAY 50

The best way to avoid disappointment
is to not expect anything from anyone

| |
| |
| |
| |
| |
| |
| |
| |

DAY 51

You never appreciate what you have
until it's gone.
A good example....toilet paper

DAY 52

People try to leave you in the cold,
but act funny when you learn to warm
up on your own

DAY 53

Most people who are loud have the
least to say

| |
| |
| |
| |
| |
| |
| |
| |

DAY 54

To love who you are, you can't hate
what you been through

DAY 55

Don't limit your challenges, challenge
your limits

DAY 56

Humble yourself or the universe will

DAY 57

People will quit on you; you gotta get up every day with the attitude that you will not quit on yourself

DAY 58

Every next level of life will need a
different version of you

<table>
<tr><td></td></tr>
<tr><td></td></tr>
<tr><td></td></tr>
<tr><td></td></tr>
<tr><td></td></tr>
<tr><td></td></tr>
<tr><td></td></tr>
<tr><td></td></tr>
</table>

DAY 59

Nothing haunts you like things you
never tried to do

DAY 60

Most times in life you learn lessons,
it's only sometimes in life that you
apply those lessons

DAY 61

Your goal should scare you a little and
excite you a whole lot

DAY 62

There are way too many things to make
you happy,
don't focus time on things that make
you sad

DAY 63

Like a nickel and a dime....
sometimes your circle is smaller and
has more value

| |
| |
| |
| |
| |
| |
| |
| |

DAY 64

Hustle hard enough that your haters
start asking
if you know who's hiring

DAY 65

Don't go broke trying to look rich

| |
| |
| |
| |
| |
| |
| |
| |

DAY 66

Continuous improvement is better than
delayed perfection

DAY 67

People can't understand your grind if
they don't have your vision

DAY 68

Your new life will probably cost you
your old life

DAY 69

You can get fired from your job, you can't get fired from your gift ...find your gift and you'll always have an opportunity to work

DAY 70

Your apology needs to be as loud as
your disrespect

<table>
<tr><td></td></tr>
<tr><td></td></tr>
<tr><td></td></tr>
<tr><td></td></tr>
<tr><td></td></tr>
<tr><td></td></tr>
<tr><td></td></tr>
<tr><td></td></tr>
</table>

DAY 71

You can't heal in the same environment
that you got sick in

| |
| |
| |
| |
| |
| |
| |
| |

DAY 72

When you know better, do better!

DAY 73

Excuses don't build empires

DAY 74

Be loyal...but don't be stupid

DAY 75

It's funny how the mind works, it's like a
parachute...
it doesn't work unless it's open

DAY 76

Never forget your own worth

DAY 77

A lion never has to explain that it's a lion

DAY 78

People can only stomach the truth
when it's the flavor they like

DAY 79

Climb the mountain so you can see the
world,
not so the world can see you

DAY 80

People with good intentions make
promises,
people with good character keep them

DAY 81

When your mind is made up and
focused you don't make excuses. You
try, if you fail...you try again

DAY 82

Dress how you want to be addressed

DAY 83

Gotta move different when you want different

DAY 84

When you're a loser you hope other
people lose

DAY 85

Don't miss out on something amazing,
because it's difficult

DAY 86

One of the most expensive things is to
pay attention to the wrong people

DAY 87

No one ever know when you're being
provoked,
only when you retaliate

DAY 88

Focus on getting better and everything
around you will get better

DAY 89

If you fail to plan, you can plan to fail

DAY 90

If I love you, I have to make you
conscious of things you don't see

DAY 91

Stay positive, work hard and make it happen

DAY 92

Pay close attention to those who don't
clap when you win

DAY 93

On a mission, your worst enemy is idle
time

DAY 94

Our lives begin to end the day we
become silent
about things that matter

DAY 95

Stop asking blind people to see your vision

DAY 96

Communication destroys assumption

DAY 97

Just because you look good, don't mean
you're a good look

DAY 98

Your greatest challenges in life come
from subtle places

DAY 99

Sometimes peace is better than trying
to be right

DAY 100

Some people don't like you because
you're the example
or what they could've been

DAY 101

Forgiveness is not a moment, it's a journey

DAY 102

Learn to accept the apology you never got

DAY 103

A listening ear can also be a running mouth

DAY 104

If you shine too much, they won't root
for you;
if you struggle too much, they won't
believe you

DAY 105

Starve your distractions, feed your focus

DAY 106

You gotta get up every day and
make sure you never quit on yourself

DAY 107

Nothing will work, unless you do

DAY 108

When someone shows you who they
are believe them

DAY 109

Everyone wants to be a beast until it's
time to do what beast do

DAY 110

Nothing plus nothing will never equal something,
it will always equal nothing.....do something!

DAY 111

If you get the inside right, the outside
will fall into place

DAY 112

Always do the right thing even when no one is looking

DAY 113

Don't ruin a good today by thinking
about a bad yesterday

DAY 114

Don't get mad, get a better
understanding of who you're dealing
with and make the proper adjustments

DAY 115

You always get tested before getting to
the next level

DAY 116

If you don't make mistakes you haven't
reached far enough

DAY 117

Be somebody nobody thought you
could be

DAY 118

The bad news is, nothing last forever.
The good news is, nothing last forever

DAY 119

Some people will never like you
because
your spirit irritates their demon

DAY 120

When you become friends of other like-minded powerful people, you shine brighter

| |
| |
| |
| |
| |
| |
| |
| |

DAY 121

Help someone to change a life, not for
reward

DAY 122

Just because it's free, don't mean it
won't cost you

DAY 123

Never let your emotions overpower
your intelligence

| |
| |
| |
| |
| |
| |
| |
| |

DAY 124

Have the courage to be disliked

DAY 125

Be a good person but don't waste time
to prove it

DAY 126

I changed my thinking, it changed my life

DAY 127

Lack of consistency can bring lack of interest

DAY 128

Value anyone who values you with
nothing to gain

DAY 129

Climb the mountain so you can see the
world,
not so the world can see you

| |
| |
| |
| |
| |
| |
| |
| |
| |

DAY 130

Some of the loudest people have the least to say

| |
| |
| |
| |
| |
| |
| |
| |

DAY 131

Your best teacher is your last mistake

DAY 132

Pay attention to how people treat you
around others

DAY 133

I changed my thinking, it changed my life

DAY 134

Sometimes what is meant for you can't
find you
because you're not being yourself

DAY 135

Stop feeding into things that are eating
you up

DAY 136

They are way ore things that make you
happy,
so don't focus on the things that make
you sad

DAY 137

You are your only limit

DAY 138

You are not what happened to you,
you are what you choose to become

DAY 139

Maturity is learning to walk away

| |
| |
| |
| |
| |
| |
| |
| |

DAY 140

Mindset is what separates the best
from the best

DAY 141

You may not be there yet but you're
closer
than you were yesterday

DAY 142

Coming together is a beginning, keeping together is a progress, working together is success

DAY 143

Never trust your fears, they don't know
your strengths

DAY 144

Never let what you're hearing about
somebody change how you view them;
you might be hearing it from a hater

DAY 145

You're only powerless if you believe it

DAY 146

Your greatest test will be how you
handle people
who mishandled you

| |
| |
| |
| |
| |
| |
| |
| |

DAY 147

Integrity is doing the right thing when
nobody is looking

DAY 148

The only person you are destined to
become
is the person that you decide to be

DAY 149

One small crack doesn't mean you're
broken,
it means you didn't break

DAY 150

Don't confuse the length of the
friendship to be the
strength of the friendship

DAY 151

Don't hold on and speak on your
weaknesses,
everyone else is already doing that for
you

DAY 152

Growth is often mistaken with acting
funny

DAY 153

You can't see peace until you are at peace

DAY 154

Everything is a blessing; it just depends
on how you look at it

DAY 155

I show my scars so others know they can heal

DAY 156

The best way to avoid disappointment,
is not to expect it

DAY 157

Remember that still voice, listen to it

DAY 158

Failure is a bruise not a tattoo

DAY 159

You have to be odd to be number one

DAY 160

Pay attention to what people tell you
out of anger,
they been waiting to tell you that

DAY 161

Your only limit is your mind

DAY 162

When it's your turn I hope you
understand
why the wait was necessary

DAY 163

Don't ignore the signs you asked God to
show you

DAY 164

If you fall seven times, make sure you
get up eight times

DAY 165

If someone offers you an amazing opportunity and you're not sure if you can do it, say yes and learn how to do it later

| |
| |
| |
| |
| |
| |
| |
| |
| |

DAY 166

Sleeping on yourself is never part of the
dream

DAY 167

Be who you needed when you were younger

DAY 168

Your dreams are calling, WAKE UP!

DAY 169

It cost you nothing to believe in
yourself....
but it will cost you everything if you
don't

DAY 170

You are allowed to change

DAY 171

Pay attention to people actions,
they say they speak louder than words

DAY 172

A child educated only at school, is an
uneducated child

DAY 173

Never let your loyalty make a fool of
you

DAY 174

365 new days, 365 new chances

DAY 175

Don't judge a situation you never been in

DAY 176

It's going to be hard but hard doesn't
mean impossible

DAY 177

Never be embarrassed to say you
struggled

DAY 178

People say a lot, so watch what they do

DAY 179

The creative adult is the child who
survived

DAY 180

A goal without a deadline is just a vision

| |
| |
| |
| |
| |
| |
| |
| |

DAY 181

Their opinion is not your reality

DAY 182

Not all storms come to disrupt your life,
some come to clear your path

DAY 183

Don't confuse who you're around with
who is on your side,
there's a big difference

DAY 184

Become more aware of what's really
worth your energy

DAY 185

Trust the vibes you get, energy doesn't lie

DAY 186

You be you and let the world adjust

DAY 187

Dreams don't work unless you do

DAY 188

If you have a heartbeat you still have
time for your dreams

DAY 189

It's not how long you live, it's how well
you live

DAY 190

A Lion doesn't turn around when a dog bark

| |
| |
| |
| |
| |
| |
| |
| |

DAY 191

A man is great not because he hasn't failed,
a man is great because failure hasn't stopped him

DAY 192

Use your pain to push your greatness

DAY 193

Don't use your energy to worry, use
your energy to believe

DAY 194

You have to learn to get up from the
table
when it's no longer being served with
love

DAY 195

Surround yourself around people who
talk
about visions and ideas, not people

DAY 196

Your name is in rooms that you haven't
even entered yet

DAY 197

Loyalty is about people who stay true
behind your back

DAY 198

Be careful not to hurt who was sent
your way

DAY 199

No response is a response, and it's a powerful one

DAY 200

Eliminate what doesn't help you evolve

DAY 201

An apology without change is just
manipulation

DAY 202

Efforts speak louder than words

DAY 203

Don't let what you're doing be
influenced by
someone who's not even on your level

DAY 204

If you scared to do it, do it scared!

DAY 205

When you get it, help someone else get it

DAY 206

Don't forget to breathe, no one can
breathe for you

DAY 207

When you're good at something you'll
tell everyone,
but when you're great they'll tell you

DAY 208

You can't bring medicine to those that
want to stay sick

DAY 209

To manifest it, you must believe in its
inevitability

DAY 210

Learn to live comfortable with being
uncomfortable!
Don't be stagnant in your
comfortability!

| |
| |
| |
| |
| |
| |
| |
| |

DAY 211

A mistake repeated more than once is a
decision

DAY 212

Just because you hear the horn honking
doesn't mean it's for you to slow down

DAY 213

In your life, positivity+positivity can
only add value to you

DAY 214

Respect commands itself and can
neither be given
or held when it is due

DAY 215

You have to be sure to be silent in order
to listen,
notice they're spelled with the same
letters

DAY 216

The most powerful thing you can do
right now is be patient
while things are unfolding for you

DAY 217

Success is the true sum of small efforts
repeated day in and day out

DAY 218

When people don't move like you do,
your ambition can sound like arrogance

DAY 219

Gotta move different when you want
different

DAY 220

The #1 source of motivation each day is
waking up

DAY 221

Stop getting distracted by things that
have
nothing to do with your goals

DAY 222

Of course, you'll struggle, just don't quit

DAY 223

Don't talk, just act; don't say, just show;
don't promise, just prove

DAY 224

You gotta know how dope you are
without validation, congratulation or
celebration

DAY 225

Don't let social media harm your
mental health

DAY 226

Don't let people in the back row help
you
make a front row decision

DAY 227

You gotta want it more than they don't
want you to have it

DAY 228

Don't decrease your goal, increase your effort

DAY 229

Not everyone deserves the real you,
let them criticize who they think you
are

DAY 230

It's you vs. you, make sure you win!

DAY 231

Healing can be a choice; how long that takes never is

DAY 232

Believe in your abilities more than you
believe in your excuses

DAY 233

Don't be afraid to go out on a limb,
that's where the fruit is

DAY 234

The best part about waking up, is
waking up

DAY 235

Always ask....

DAY 236

If you don't have big dreams and big
goals,
you'll end up working really hard for
someone who does

DAY 237

It's ok to clap for someone if their
dream takes off before yours

_____
_____
_____
_____
_____
_____
_____
_____

DAY 238

No matter how you feel....get up, dress
up,
show up and never give up

DAY 239

Grow through what you go through

DAY 240

Vision isn't just eyesight but insight and foresight

DAY 241

Happy people ain't hating

DAY 242

Get in the habit of asking yourself,
"does this support the life I'm trying to
create"

DAY 243

Your patience when you have nothing is
your attitude when you have everything

DAY 244

You've got the time

DAY 245

Tell the truth or someone will tell it for you

DAY 246

Small minds will never understand a big mission

| |
| |
| |
| |
| |
| |
| |
| |

DAY 247

Stop expecting you from other people

DAY 248

Don't get upset with people and
situations
because both are powerless without
your reaction

DAY 249

It's the will not the skill

DAY 250

Your plan should be your dream on
paper;
don't just think it, ink it

DAY 251

Clever is not the same as true

DAY 252

You gotta start hanging out with people
who fit your future,
not your history

DAY 253

Cut yourself some slack, you're doing
better than you think

DAY 254

When you are sleep you have dreams,
when you are woke you have visions

DAY 255

Some people won't like you, and you
will live with that

DAY 256

Don't blame a clown for being a clown, blame yourself for keep going to the circus

DAY 257

The biggest risk you take is not taking
one

DAY 258

Some people try to disturb your peace
and they're at war with themselves

DAY 259

Always strive to be better than who you
were yesterday

DAY 260

Be addicted to yourself

| |
| |
| |
| |
| |
| |
| |
| |

DAY 261

Starve your distractions and feed your focus

DAY 262

The only place that success comes
before work is the dictionary

DAY 263

Painful lessons are permanent lessons

DAY 264

Your biggest hater is never a stranger

| |
| |
| |
| |
| |
| |
| |
| |

DAY 265

Sometimes you win, sometimes you learn

DAY 266

When you get it, help someone else get
it

DAY 267

Don't develop feelings for distractions

DAY 268

Your new life is going to cost you your old one

DAY 269

Relax, you're still growing

DAY 270

Either they grow with you or you
outgrow them,
don't stand still for anyone

DAY 271

Every next level of your life will demand
a different you

DAY 272

Don't get upset with people,
they are powerless without your
reaction

DAY 273

You can't stop 6 a.m. from coming,
tomorrow will be here waiting on you,
go get it done

DAY 274

Some will, some won't, so what!

DAY 275

Always stand for what's right even if
you're standing alone

DAY 276

Be in love with your life, every minute
of it

DAY 277

Grow where you are planted

DAY 278

If you don't guard your time people will waste it

DAY 279

One day or day one? You decide!

DAY 280

Are your values aligned with your goals
and dreams?

DAY 281

In order for them to bring you down,
they have to be able to reach you

DAY 282

Negativity can only affect you if you're
on that frequency

DAY 283

Don't try to change anyone,
change how you deal with them

| |
| |
| |
| |
| |
| |
| |
| |

DAY 284

Don't let yesterday take too much of today

DAY 285

Time you enjoy wasting is not time
wasted

DAY 286

Don't be busy, be productive

DAY 287

Be a good person but don't waste time
to prove it

DAY 288

Tomorrow you will wish you had
started today

DAY 289

Take massive action and you'll get
massive results

DAY 290

The mission you're on is personal, you owe it to yourself

DAY 291

Do good and good will come to you

DAY 292

I order to start "ballin" you have to b-all-in

DAY 293

Be happy with what you have while
working for what you want

DAY 294

If your mind can't picture your future it
will only replay your past

| |
| |
| |
| |
| |
| |
| |
| |

DAY 295

Conflict cannot survive when only one
person participates

DAY 296

Surround yourself with people who talk
about visions and ideas, not people

DAY 297

You can be anything you want in this
world,
just don't be ungrateful

DAY 298

Make sure you focus on unity when
doing for the commUNITY

DAY 299

Do what others aren't willing to do, so
you can do what they can't

DAY 300

Until you take a BIG chance in life,
you never really know how BIG you are
(Mika sent this)

DAY 301

Your problem isn't your problem, your
problem is your reaction

DAY 302

Don't quit your daydream

DAY 303

It didn't come to consume you, it came
to develop you

DAY 304

Success consist of going from failure to
failure without loss of enthusiasm

DAY 305

Sometimes you need to ask for
forgiveness
instead of asking for permission

DAY 306

Certain levels in life will require more
alone time

DAY 307

Stop expecting you from other people

DAY 308

The standards you set determine the life
you get

| |
| |
| |
| |
| |
| |
| |
| |

DAY 309

You're the CEO of your life! Hire, fire and
promote accordingly

DAY 310

Don't regret anything that you needed to learn

DAY 311

Many people love the idea of you but lack
the maturity
to handle the reality of you

DAY 312

Be somebody who makes everybody feel
like somebody

DAY 313

Never apologize for who you are

DAY 314

Stop chasing people and things that aren't
meant for you

DAY 315

Stop acting like you live twice

DAY 316

When people sleep on you, let them get their rest

DAY 317

History doesn't talk about quitters

DAY 318

To be a leader you must be able to make an
idea reality

DAY 319

Don't wait for your dreams to come true,
come true to your dreams

DAY 320

Don't lose alone because your too insecure
to win together

DAY 321

The difference between a goal and a dream,
is a plan

DAY 322

Be the reason someone believes in the
goodness of people

DAY 323

The meaning of life is to find your gift,
the purpose of life is to give it away

DAY 324

You change the view of your perception,
you change your reality

DAY 325

Challenge your fears and attempt the things
that people say are impossible

DAY 326

Don't be afraid to close your eyes to dream,
just be sure to open your eyes to see

DAY 327

Whatever you are not changing in your life,
you are choosing

DAY 328

One of your goals should be not to be
better than anyone
but be better than you were yesterday

DAY 329

There are too many ants telling bees how to make honey

DAY 330

Silence is an answer too

DAY 331

Surround yourself with big dreamers

DAY 332

Success equals sacrifice, what are you
willing to give up

DAY 333

Don't ask people who never been where
you've been for directions

DAY 334

The quieter you become, the more you can
hear

DAY 335

Control how you respond to things that
destroy your peace

DAY 336

You are what you do, not what you say
you'll do

DAY 337

The sun is alone, but it still shines

DAY 338

You can approach a problem with a solution
or a complaint,
it's your choice

DAY 339

Never be too embarrassed to say you're struggling

DAY 340

Be crazy enough to know that you can do
whatever you want with your life

DAY 341

The best project you'll ever work on is YOU

| |
| |
| |
| |
| |
| |
| |
| |

DAY 342

Don't confuse the length of your
relationship
with the strength of your relationship

| |
| |
| |
| |
| |
| |
| |
| |

DAY 343

Be too busy working on your grass
that you forget to notice that theirs is
greener

DAY 344

Why would you question what you know is right

DAY 345

If at first you don't succeed......tuck your chin,
keep going and continue to be great

DAY 346

It's not the problem that's the problem,
it's that lack of solutions to the
problem... that's the problem

DAY 347

There is only one person that YOU are
in control of.....

DAY 348

What you see is not what you get,
what you want to see is what you
choose to get

DAY 349

Love should not hurt;
pain is a consequence of love, not a
part of love

DAY 350

1+1 does not always equal 2....
depending on the views of your teacher
it could equal 11

DAY 351

Who you are in your mind could get you
further
than your mind could ever imagine

DAY 352

In case of emergencies put your mask on first before helping others...read it again

DAY 353

As long as you keep one foot in front of the
other,
you will always be walking

DAY 354

Sometimes to put the fire out you need
to know what kind of fire you are
approaching

DAY 355

Family is family, you can't change
that....
family is also friends who change what
your family can look like

DAY 356

You start how you finish

DAY 357

Be proud of your work,
you're the first person to show interest
in it

DAY 358

Pay attention to your friends who are
not cheering for you while on your way
up

DAY 359

Some of the most beautiful things are
on the opposite side of fear

DAY 360

Love your family, they're yours for a
reason

DAY 361

Say it, forget it...
write it or regret it

DAY 362

You can buy good things – good food,
good clothes, good entertainment; you
can't buy great, greatness is in you

DAY 363

If you have to talk to more than three
people about the same problem, you
don't have a problem, you want
attention

DAY 364

You are in charge, don't wait for a
perfect time;
there's no better time to start than now

DAY 365

Today marks 365 days of positive
messages from me to you,
1 whole year! So I want to end it with
this –

Keep Living......

"LIVE IT UP"
Friday's are great, a day before the
weekend.
What if every day felt like Friday,
it can if you do what you need to be
happy with life.

PEACE!
-BJ Paige

www.ingramcontent.com/pod-product-compliance
Lightning Source LLC
Chambersburg PA
CBHW061041110426
42740CB00050B/2524